When Mommy Loves Bama and Daddy Loves Auburn

by
Deb Hiett

Illustrations by
Amy Lynn Stevenson

ISBN: 978-0-9894352-0-8

   1.   Humor.

Published by Sweet Biscuit Productions
www.SweetBiscuitProductions.com

This is a work of fiction. Names, characters, businesses, places, events, and incidents are either the products of the author's imagination or used in a fictitious manner and for literary effect only.

That said, all the food mentioned in this book is truly delicious.

Dedicated to all the children
who learn "SEC" before "ABC"

During the fall, Saturday is our
favorite day of the week.

In the morning, we must
do our chores.

Then the fun begins.
We change into our
football-watching clothes!
We're so lucky because
we get to wear
crimson and white AND
orange and **blue**.

Want to know why?

Because
MOMMY
loves
BAMA
and
DADDY
loves
AUBURN!

Some people we know say *either*
"ROLL TIDE ROLL!" *or*
"WAR EAGLE!" We're lucky
because we get to say both.

Once when we were little, we got mixed up
and said "Roll Eagle!" and "War Tide!" It made
us laugh and laugh, but Mommy got one of her
headaches and had to leave the room.

We always root for Alabama and Auburn
whenever they play another team.
Here are the rules about who we
cheer for in our special house:

Who we cheer for:
#1 alabaMa + aubuM
#2 no one else *

*There is an exception to rule number two, which is when Steve Spurrier is head coach somewhere. Then we have to cheer for whoever is playing Steve Spurrier's team.

We are not sure why.

It's important that we have exactly
the right snacks for Game Day, like
Niffer's Corn Nugget and Fried Pickle Combo
and The Globe's Grilled Cheese sandwiches
with Tri-Color Chips and Toomer's Drug Store
Lemonade and Dreamland Bar-B-Que.
We're so lucky!

Daddy says, "Food is love" and
"My belt shrunk" and
"Let's see if *this* beer will do it."
He is so funny.

But there is one special Saturday when
Alabama and Auburn play each other.
That game is called The Iron Bowl.

We do NOT like it.

We do NOT like The Iron Bowl Day
because Mommy and Daddy
send us away for the game.

Once we went over to Dr. Valenti's house next
door, and Dr. Valenti tried to explain why
"It's important to be Switzerland."

One year Mommy and Daddy sent us to
Preacher Jeff's place for The Iron Bowl Day.
When we told Preacher Jeff that we had once
accidentally said "ROLL EAGLE" and
"WAR TIDE," he tried to explain
what a "blasphemy" is and
why it makes Jesus so sad.

Last year, Mommy and Daddy sent us to Uncle Bill's apartment for The Iron Bowl Day. Uncle Bill went on and on about his plan to reform the BCS, whether or not Paul Finebaum is a leader in the Illuminati, and why we need to "follow the money" to get to the bottom of "the Notre Dame rule."

But this year, we sneaked away
to our secret backyard tent.

We could hear the sounds of
The Iron Bowl coming through
the den windows.

The marching bands sounded like
a *billion* bucks.

The crowds were roaring so loud that
our den door kept slamming shut.

Verne Lundquist must have been
cracking lots of jokes, because
Mommy kept shouting,
"OH YOU HAVE GOT TO BE
KIDDIN' ME."

Plus we learned lots and lots
of new words!

Lucky, lucky us!

Every year on The Iron Bowl Day,
one of our two favorite teams wins, and
one of our parents is very happy.

The other parent was "robbed" and
announces plans to write
"a strongly-worded letter" about
"investigating biased refs" or
"firing that idiot." We've learned to
"enjoy it while you can" or
"just wait until next year"
and sometimes
"help Daddy to the toilet."

Usually, Alabama or Auburn is in
another bowl game later, but the
winner of The Iron Bowl matters most.
That's why we're so lucky!
We ALWAYS have the winner
in our house, because...

Mommy loves Bama
and
Daddy loves Auburn!

THE END

ABOUT THE ILLUSTRATOR

Originally from Holdrege, Nebraska, Amy Lynn earned a B.F.A. from the University of Nebraska at Kearney in 1995. Then she moved to Minneapolis, where she worked as an artist for almost nine years. In 2004, Amy Lynn moved to Los Angeles. With one exhibit after another, art critics hailed her as "one to watch" and she was soon featured in leading art publications such as *Art Collectors Magazine* and *Art World News*. She was commissioned to do a series of paintings for the Kyoto Grand Hotel in Los Angeles. Her artwork has been prominently featured on television, including the FOX hit, "Hell's Kitchen." In 2011, she became a Disney Fine Artist and is producing her own originals and limited editions with Collector's Editions and Disney Fine Art, which are shown in Disney Galleries Worldwide.

See more of Amy Lynn's talents at
amylynnpaints.com.

ABOUT THE AUTHOR

Writer/actress Deb Hiett was raised in a happy "house divided" in Birmingham, where both the Crimson Tide and the Auburn Tigers are cheered. After years of performing and writing in New York City, Deb moved to Los Angeles where her short comedy film, "A Bit of Counseling" (co-written and performed with Richard Kuhlman), won the Audience Choice Awards at the Palm Beach International Film Festival and the L.A. Comedy Shorts Film Festival. Deb has created and performed two one-woman comedy shows, in New York (*Village Voice* called her "the bold new voice in solo . . . a sure-shot writer") and at The Second City in Los Angeles. She has appeared as an actress on "Arrested Development," "Parks and Recreation," "The Office," "Desperate Housewives," "Prison Break," "Boston Legal," and "Real Time with Bill Maher," among other television shows and films. In addition to writing and performing, Deb soothes her Southern homesickness by growing her own collards, okra, and watermelon. She's also been known to play the accordion.

Read more at <u>DebHiett.com</u>
and follow her @debhiett on Twitter.

CPSIA information can be obtained
at www.ICGtesting.com
Printed in the USA
LVIC04n2115200913
353471LV00033B

* 9 7 8 0 9 8 9 4 3 5 2 0 8 *